Consciousness And Self-Consciousness

H. P. Blavatsky

Kessinger Publishing's Rare Reprints

Thousands of Scarce and Hard-to-Find Books on These and other Subjects!

- Americana
- Ancient Mysteries
- Animals
- Anthropology
- Architecture
- Arts
- Astrology
- Bibliographies
- Biographies & Memoirs
- Body, Mind & Spirit
- Business & Investing
- Children & Young Adult
- Collectibles
- Comparative Religions
- Crafts & Hobbies
- Earth Sciences
- Education
- Ephemera
- Fiction
- Folklore
- Geography
- Health & Diet
- History
- Hobbies & Leisure
- Humor
- Illustrated Books
- Language & Culture
- Law
- Life Sciences
- Literature
- Medicine & Pharmacy
- Metaphysical
- Music
- Mystery & Crime
- Mythology
- Natural History
- Outdoor & Nature
- Philosophy
- Poetry
- Political Science
- Science
- Psychiatry & Psychology
- Reference
- Religion & Spiritualism
- Rhetoric
- Sacred Books
- Science Fiction
- Science & Technology
- Self-Help
- Social Sciences
- Symbolism
- Theatre & Drama
- Theology
- Travel & Explorations
- War & Military
- Women
- Yoga
- *Plus Much More!*

**We kindly invite you to view our catalog list at:
http://www.kessinger.net**

THIS ARTICLE WAS EXTRACTED FROM THE BOOK:

Theosophist Magazine July 1925-September 1925

BY THIS AUTHOR:

H. P. Blavatsky

ISBN 0766151824

READ MORE ABOUT THE BOOK AT OUR WEB SITE:

http://www.kessinger.net

OR ORDER THE COMPLETE
BOOK FROM YOUR FAVORITE STORE

ISBN 0766151824

CONSCIOUSNESS AND SELF-CONSCIOUSNESS

By H. P. BLAVATSKY

[The following is evidently a rough commencement of an article in H.P.B.'s handwriting in the T. S. Records. It is printed exactly as she wrote it.—C.J.]

THE *cycle* of consciousness. It is argued that there cannot be more than one object of perception at a time before the soul because soul is a unit. Occultism teaches that simultaneously our conscious[ness] could receive no less than *seven* distinct impressions, and even pass them into memory. This can be proved by striking at the same time seven keys of the scale of an instrument—say a piano. The 7 sounds will reach consciousness simultaneously; though the untrained consciousness may not be capable of registering them the first second, their prolonged vibrations will strike the ear in 7 distinct sounds one higher than the other in its pitch. All depends on training and attention. Thus the transference of a sensation from any organ to consciousness is almost instantaneous if your attention is fixed upon it; but if any noise distracts your attention it will take a number of seconds before it reaches consciousness. The Occultist should train himself to receive and transmit along the line of the seven scales of his consciousness every impression or impressions simultaneously. He who reduces the intervals of physical time the most, has made the most progress.

The names and order of the 7 scales are.

1. Sense-perception;
2. Self-perception (or apperception)
3. Psychic apperception—which carries it to
4. Vital perception.

These are the four lower scales and belong to the psycho physical man. The[n] come

5. Manasic discernment;
6. Will perception and
7. Spiritual conscious apperception.

The special organ of consciousness is of course the brain, and is located in the aura of the pineal gland in the living man. During the process of mind or thought manifesting to consciousness, constant vibrations of light take place. If one could see clairvoyantly in the brain of a living man one could almost count (see with the eye) the seven shades of the successive scales of light, from the dullest to the brightest.

What consciousness *is* can never be defined psychologically. We can analyse and classify its work and effects—we cannot define it, unless we postulate an Ego distinct from the body. The septenary scale of states of consciousness is reflected in the heart, or rather its area[1], which vibrates and illumines the *seven brains* of the heart as it does the seven divisions or rays around the pineal gland.

This consc[iousness] shows to us the difference between the nature and essence of, say, astral body and Ego. One molecular, invisible unless condensed, the other atomic-spiritual. (See example of smoker—ten cigarettes the smoke of each retaining its affinity.

---

[1] Word difficult to decipher; may be intended for "aura," though it looks like "area".—C.J.

Idea of Ego the only one compatible with the facts of physiological observation.

The mind or Ego, the *subject* of all and every state of consciousness is essentially a unity. The millions of various sub-states of consc[iousness] are a proof of the existence of this Ego. Even the brain cells furnish us with those states which affirm to us that there is an immortal soul etc.

Every one of the five recognized senses was primarily a mental sense. A fish born in a cave is blind—let it out into a river and it will begin to *feel* it sees, until gradually the physical organ of sight evolves and it will see. A deaf and dumb man hears *internally*, in his own way. Knowing feeling willing not faculties of mind—its colleagues (p. 631.)

[H. P. Blavatsky]

B
105
.C477
B5

SOUTH UNIVERSITY LIBRARY